THE GOLDEN YEARS

1971

text: David Sandison

design: Paul Kurzeja

SIENA

Welcome to The Golden Years and the people, places, achievements and events which made 1971 so special. It was special for US astronauts James Irwin and David Scott, who went driving on the moon; for Princess Anne, whose equestrian skills earned her Britain's Sportswoman of the Year title; for the people of Haiti, as dictator François 'Papa Doc' Duvalier died and for the people of East Pakistan, whose attempts to establish the independent state of Bangladesh would trigger a terrible reign of terror by West Pakistani troops.

While the legendary Rolls-Royce company went broke, British politicians decided to go for membership of the European Common Market, and Libya went for broke when it seized all £80 million of BP's assets.

The music world lost the genius of Louis Armstrong and Igor Stravinsky. Uganda gained a new President in the shape of former army boxing champion Idi Amin, and Winnie Mandela - keeping on the fight for black Africans' rights while her husband spent his

seventh year in prison - found herself sentenced to a year's incarceration.

President Richard Nixon bowed to the inevitable and did not use his veto to block Mao Tse-Tung's mainland China finally joining the United Nations, and nobody really mourned the passing, in disgrace and obscurity, of former Soviet leader Nikita Khrushchev. There were tears for the first British soldier to die on the streets of Ulster as that sorry and tragic drama continued to claim victims on all sides.

It's all here - and a lot more besides. Enjoy!

JAN

Ibrox Tragedy: 66 Killed As Barriers Collapse

NEW YEAR CELEBRATIONS turned to tragedy in Glasgow today when 66 soccer fans were killed during a game between the city's deadly rivals, Glasgow Rangers and Glasgow Celtic. As home fans surged forwards to greet an equalizing goal by their team, barriers buckled and collapsed, and hundreds of people were submerged beneath a tangle of fallen bodies.

As an official inquiry was initiated into British football's worst disaster to date, it became clear that the incident happened as hundreds of Rangers fans who'd begun to leave the ground as the match neared its end, raced back to be part of the joy which marked the Rangers goal. The sheer weight of numbers pushing forward from the back toppled those further down the terrace, some of whom were forced onto the pitch. The pressure proved too much for steel safety barriers and the inevitable happened.

After police, ambulance workers and fellow fans had forced their way through the tangle of bodies, 66 were found to be dead and 150 injured, some of them seriously.

JANUARY 10

Fashion World Mourns Style Queen 'Coco'

French fashion legend 'Coco' Chanel died today in her suite at the Paris Ritz, leaving a huge gap in the industry she had helped to transform in the 1920s with the simple, elegant suits and dresses she designed to liberate a generation of women from the confines of corsets and stays.

Aged 87, but believed by many to be immortal, Chanel also introduced bobbed hair, and made costume jewellery and suntans fashionable. She also made a fortune with her No 5 perfume, so called because that was her 'lucky' number.

There was nothing lucky about her rise and continued dominance of the notoriously fickle world of fashion. Shrewd and ruthless, the beautiful but resolutely single 'Coco' built her empire with care and craft, just as she created the styles which made her name synonymous with French chic.

JANUARY 8

Uruguay Rebels Kidnap British Envoy

The British Ambassador to Uruguay, Mr Geoffrey Jackson, was kidnapped today in the capital, Montevideo, by members of the left-wing Tupamaros guerrilla movement. While accomplices staged a diversionary incident to attract police to another part of the city, five cars forced the 53 year old ambassador's limousine off the road and pushed him at gun-point into one of their vehicles.

Uruguay had been a notoriously dangerous posting for some time - an American agricultural expert and a Brazilian diplomat were already being held hostage by the Tupamaros. In London, the Foreign Office confirmed that their anxiety over Mr Jackson's fate was compounded by the fact that he suffered from a heart condition.

While a number of suspects were rounded up as 12,000 Uruguayan police and army officers began an all-out search of the Montevideo area, Mr Jackson's whereabouts remained a mystery.

UK TOP 10 SINGLES

1: Grandad
- Clive Dunn
2: I Hear You Knocking
- Dave Edmunds
3: Ride A White Swan
- T Rex
4: I'll Be There
- The Jackson Five
5: When I'm Dead And Gone
- McGuinness Flint
6: Cracklin' Rosie
- Neil Diamond
7: Blame It On The Pony Express
- Johnny Johnson & The Bandwagon
8: It's Only Make Believe
- Glen Campbell
9: Ape Man
- The Kinks
10: Home Lovin' Man
- Andy Williams

JANUARY 25

Manson Family Found Guilty Of Tate Murders

In Los Angeles, today, Charles Manson (pictured), the leader of a murderous hippy 'family' who claimed that secret messages on Beatles' records had confirmed that he should wage a race and class war to help hasten the arrival of Armageddon, was convicted of the murders of the pregnant actress Sharon Tate and four others at her Beverly Hills home in August 1969, and of the killing of a wealthy couple, the LaBiancas, the following night. Also convicted were the three members of Manson's gruesome collection of misfits who actually carried out his orders - Susan Atkins, Leslie Van Houten and Patricia Krenwinkel. During the 121-day trial, which dominated US and world news media every bit as much as the recent OJ Simpson hearings, Manson veered between casual disdain of the court and apparent disinterest in the often horrific evidence, to wild rantings to justify his actions. Although Manson would be sentenced to death, California's suspension of the death penalty would mean he'd be sentenced to life without parole.
Manson and other followers would also be convicted of three other murders at later trials.

JANUARY 12

British Minister's House Bombed By Angry Brigade

A MASSIVE NATIONWIDE police and security services investigation was launched in Britain tonight when the north London home of Robert Carr, the Secretary of State for Employment, was wrecked by two time bombs planted by an extremist group calling itself The Angry Brigade.

Although Mr Carr, his wife and daughter were in the house when the bombs exploded, they all escaped unharmed as windows were shattered, the front door was blown off its hinges, and the minister's official Daimler car was damaged by flying debris.

While security forces must have had well-founded suspicions of just who was responsible for the outrage, speculation in British newspapers ended just two days later when an unsigned letter arrived at the offices of all major dailies, admitting that The Angry Brigade had carried out the attack.

The group, which had previously claimed responsibility for planting bombs near a BBC outside broadcast van during the Miss World contest, machine-gunning the Spanish Embassy in London, and attempting to bomb the Department of Employment headquarters in Westminster, also wrote a longer, more specific letter to The Times on January 27, saying it was carrying out a class war against the Conservative government.

JANUARY 25

Coup Makes Idi Amin Uganda Supremo

Taking advantage of President Milton Obote's absence from Uganda while he attended a Commonwealth conference in Singapore, a combined army and police cabal led by Major-General Idi Amin today ousted the President and set up a new administration headed by the 45 year old former army boxing champion.

Accusing the former President of tribal favouritism, corruption and economic policies which guaranteed immense profits for a favoured few and abject poverty for ordinary Ugandans, Amin promised early free elections and the release of all political prisoners.

Within days Amin would order the release of 55 jailed Obote opponents, but would follow that with a ban on all political activity, dissolve Parliament, and declare himself President with supreme powers.

JANUARY 20

Britain Hit By First-Ever Post Strike

Determined that the country should not be held to ransom by the first postal strike in history, the Conservative government of Edward Heath today lifted the ban on private mail services to open the way for Britain's more enterprising entrepreneurs to keep the country in touch. The strike, which began at midnight when 230,000 postal workers walked out in protest at the rejection of their demands for a 19.5 per cent pay rise which the Post Office said would lead to an 'unacceptable' 9d (25c) letter rate.

The result? An unprecedented rush by owners of motor bikes, taxis and vans to rush around Britain, capitalizing on the crisis.

7

First British Soldier Killed In Ulster

THE BRITISH ARMY tonight suffered its first fatal casualty in the ever-increasing turmoil of sectarian warfare in Ulster when a Royal Artillery soldier, Gunner Robert Curtis, was shot and killed as his unit moved into the Ardoyne district of Belfast to break up a riot in which petrol bombers had set fire to an armoured personnel carrier.

Two civilians were also killed, and five other soldiers wounded, in the riot, which saw troops fired on by machine guns. The eight soldiers in the personnel carrier escaped unhurt.

British troops were first sent to Ulster in August 1969 in an attempt to protect a Catholic community attempting to win full political rights in a society with a Protestant-dominated constitution. The move quickly turned sour, and British forces found themselves the target for extremists on both sides of the province's political divide.

Tonight's tragic development occurred as sporadic attacks and bombings were reported throughout Northern Ireland. These included the woundings of innocent bystanders, including two girls and a boy, as gunmen opened fire from a car during the Belfast evening rush-hour.

Detectives from Scotland Yard were soon in Belfast to help local police investigate what appeared to be a second sectarian murder in as many days. In what the

authorities described as 'a sinister new development', the body of a young Protestant was dumped near Aldergrove Airport on February 8. By month end, the death toll would increase even more when, on February 26, two Belfast policemen died in hospital after being shot while on patrol.

Storm Over Powell's 'Rivers Of Blood' Speech

Conservative rebel MP Enoch Powell caused a major political storm in London this evening when, speaking in defence of the government's Immigration Bill - new legislation intended to end the right of Commonwealth workers to settle in Britain - he predicted that an uncontrolled growth in a non-white immigrant population would lead to a backlash in which he could envisage streets running in 'rivers of blood'.

Mr Powell, a classical scholar who was Professor of Greek at Sydney University before rising to the rank of Brigadier during WWII, was also putting the case for the introduction of a massive repatriation scheme for immigrants already resident in Britain. Attacked by politicians of all parties, churchmen of all denominations, civil rights organizations and the leaders of Britain's black and Asian communities, Mr Powell - MP for Wolverhampton South West since 1950 - would be forced to distance himself from the various racist groups which hailed his remarks. The damage had been done, however.

Britain Baffled As Pennies Become New Pence

Despite a multi-million pound publicity and education programme designed to make the transition as painless as possible, huge numbers of Britain's population admitted that today's switch to a new decimal currency had them at sixes and sevens.

Although the Decimal Currency Board chairman, Lord Fiske, claimed that 'all was going well', news media representatives found it all too easy to find people all too happy to moan about the hassles involved in working out just how many of the new pence they'd have to pay for goods and services which had been costed in the comfortable old way only the day before.

That old way had been amazingly complicated, with 12 old pennies to the shilling, 20 shillings to the pound, and a whole bunch of exotic coins in between - like the half-crown, which was worth two shillings and sixpence.

With one of the new pence being worth two and a half of the old pennies, that would make the half-crown worth, oh, divide by two, take away half of the number you first thought of, add two......

Swiss Women Given The Vote

It's hard to believe, especially of a modern, dynamic country in the heart of Europe, but until a referendum held today in Switzerland decided it should be so, Swiss women had not been allowed to vote in any elections.

While Swiss women quietly celebrated this long-overdue victory for common sense, the cause of universal suffrage did not fare completely well elsewhere in Europe this month.

On February 28, the exclusively male electorate of the tiny state of Liechtenstein, a close neighbour of Switzerland's, decided that allowing women to vote was all a bit progressive and risky!

ARRIVALS

Born this month:

13: Sonia, UK pop singer (*You'll Never Stop Me Loving You, Listen To Your Heart,* etc)

28: Noureddine Morceli, Algerian world 1500 metres and mile champion

South Vietnamese Attack Laos

A major offensive on communist Viet Cong positions along the Ho Chi Minh Trail - North Vietnam's principal supply route inside the neighbouring country of Laos - began today when more than 12,000 South Vietnamese troops crossed the border.

Although US forces were under strict orders not to join the South Vietnamese in Laos, the attack was aided by a heavy US artillery bombardment and air support.

Early reports said the South Vietnamese met little resistance, and captured four tanks, almost 50 trucks and a number of large arms caches on their way to their principal target of Tchepone, the Viet Cong's most important regional operations HQ.

Bankrupt Rolls-Royce Calls In The Receivers

BRITAIN'S INTERNATIONAL reputation as a centre of engineering innovation and excellence, already dented by wildcat strikes and late deliveries of exports, received its biggest blow yet today when Rolls-Royce - the acknowledged symbol of British quality and reliability - collapsed into bankruptcy and the hands of official receivers.

Brought down by a disastrous contract to design and build the RB211 jet engine for the new Lockheed Tristar plane, the Rolls-Royce bankruptcy also dealt a fatal blow to the British government's policy of returning all state industry to private ownership. Not prepared to run the risk of Rolls-Royce's strategically important aero-engine and aero-space divisions falling into foreign hands, the government would be forced to create a nationalized company, Rolls-Royce (1971) Ltd, although the luxury car division would be sold off.

Rolls-Royce's demise had been caused by the company's decision to secure the RB211 deal at all costs. The US-owned Lockheed corporation had drawn up an impossibly tough deal with severe penalty clauses and minimal profit potential. Hit by technical problems, Rolls-Royce had already been bailed out in November last year, but not even the presence of government-appointed board members could save the company from the disaster which overtook it today.

Amin: Five Years Before Elections

Only a month after grabbing power in Uganda, Major-General Idi Amin today signalled just how much his word was worth when - his new regime boosted by official British recognition on February 5 - he reneged on his early promises of early free elections and informed his people that he needed to remain in power as President for five years before elections could be held 'in a mood of tranquillity and mutual respect.' Amin hampered his chances of winning that respect by announcing that he had also promoted himself to full General, instituted a 13-point declaration to give himself almost unlimited powers, introduced severe penalties on any citizens who took part in now-banned political meetings and other activities - and said that he had ordered the return to Uganda of the body of King Freddie, the Kabaka of Uganda, who had died in London, where he'd been forced into exile by the deposed Dr Milton Obote in 1966.

Apollo 14 Astronauts Walk On Moon

Nervous NASA scientists breathed a triumphant sigh of relief in Houston today when *Apollo 14,* the latest US space mission, made a successful landing on the surface of the moon and members of the crew were able to complete a successful walk on the surface. American anxiety for the mission, and the safety of cosmonauts Roosa, Mitchell and Shepard, was founded in the near-disaster experienced last April when *Apollo 13* was hit by an explosion in its service module and the crew only just managed to return safely to earth before their air supplies were exhausted. Its launch delayed until NASA engineers were completely confident that they had eliminated all potential problems found in that near-tragedy, *Apollo 14* was launched on January 31 with an awful lot of fingers still crossed.

WAR

Bangladesh Declaration Triggers Civil War

CIVIL WAR BETWEEN East and West Pakistan - predicted as inevitable since last December's elections produced leaders with completely opposite views and objectives - became reality today when East Pakistan's Prime Minister, Sheik Mujibur Rahman, used a radio broadcast to announce the creation of the independent state of Bangladesh.

Aware that this move was imminent, West Pakistani troops had been ordered to surround six major East Pakistan towns and cities by their Prime Minister, Ali Bhutto. Fighting was reported to have broken out between opposing forces within minutes of the Sheik's broadcast.

Created by the British government in 1947 as part of the Indian Independence Act, the two halves of Pakistan were united by a shared Muslim faith, but separated by more than 1,000 miles of Indian territory and different languages. It was a botched arrangement doomed to failure from the start.

December's elections brought things to a head. West Pakistan's new PM, Ali Bhutto, was dedicated to maintain the status quo, while the Sheik - leader of the independence-seeking Awami League since 1954 - was equally dedicated to a breakaway.

The first shots in what was to become a ferocious and bloody civil war were fired in the East Pakistan/Bangladesh capital of Dhaka when West Pakistan troops tried to disarm men of the East Pakistan Rifles regiment in their barracks.

MARCH 26

Receiver's Appointment Spells End Of The Beatles

The extraordinary group called The Beatles effectively ceased to exist in law today when John Lennon, George Harrison and Ringo Starr decided not to appeal a recent High Court judgement in favour of Paul McCartney's lawsuit to wind up their company, Apple, the first step in his plan to dissolve one of the most successful musical partnerships in history.

The McCartney action, which began on January 1 with a writ demanding the break up of the partnership business known as The Beatles and Co, left the three members with legal bills estimated to be as high as £100,000 ($250,000) for close on two months of High Court hearings.

While the McCartney case concentrated on his belief that the group's affairs were being grossly mismanaged by Allen Klein, the American manager the others had appointed despite his opposition, it was an open secret that the rift which really forced the break-up was caused by the increased influence exerted by John Lennon's wife, the Japanese artist Yoko Ono.

UK TOP 10 SINGLES

1: Baby Jump
- Mungo Jerry
2: Another Day
- Paul McCartney
3: My Sweet Lord
- George Harrison
4: It's Impossible
- Perry Como
5: Rose Garden
- Lynn Anderson
6: Hot Love
- T Rex
7: The Pushbike Song
- Mixtures
8: Sweet Caroline
- Neil Diamond
9: Amazing Grace
- Judy Collins
10: Resurrection Shuffle
- Ashton, Gardner & Dyke

MARCH 1

Vietnam Protestors Bomb US Senate

Protests against US involvement in the Vietnam War, and American military support for South Vietnam's invasion of Laos three weeks ago, reached an explosive new intensity today when a bomb exploded in the Senate wing of the Capitol building in Washington DC.

Although a telephone warning ensured there were no human casualties in the blast - the first serious act of sabotage against a federal building for many years - doors were blown off their hinges, walls and floors were cracked, and windows shattered.

The person who phoned the warning specified that the bomb was a protest against the Laos action, dedicated to cutting the North Vietnamese supply line, the so-called Ho Chi Minh Trail. While the South Vietnamese forces were said to have met with little initial resistance when they invaded Laos last month, it is now known that they have been suffering heavy losses.

13

ARRIVALS

Born this month:
26: John Hendy, UK pop singer (East 17)

DEPARTURES

Died this month:
6: Pearl (Sydenstricker) Buck, US novelist (*The Good Earth, Dragon Seed,* etc), Far East missionary
8: Harold Lloyd, US comedy film actor, director *(see Came & Went pages)*
16: Thomas E Dewey, US politician, former Presidential candidate
29: Raymond William Postgate, UK historian and novelist

MARCH 3

Winnie Mandela Jailed For Receiving

Winnie Mandela, wife of the imprisoned African National Congress leader, Nelson Mandela, was herself sentenced to a year in jail by a Johannesburg court today after being found guilty of receiving visitors at her home in defiance of a government restriction order.

Mrs Mandela was released on bail pending an appeal. Under the terms of the government banning order, the 36 year old was forbidden to see anyone at her home except her two children and a family doctor. The order was designed to eliminate her vowed attempts to carry on the struggle of Nelson Mandela, jailed for conspiracy to overthrow the South African government in 1964 and serving a life sentence on Robben Island, the penal colony in Table Bay, Cape Town.

MARCH 23

Faulkner Becomes Ulster PM

As the level of violence in Ulster increased horrifically this month, with the murder of a Belfast milkman on March 7 and the deaths of three more British soldiers on March 9, the security policies of the province's Prime Minister, James Chichester-Clark, were found so wanting that his resignation, on March 20, was inevitable.

Ulster's new Prime Minister, elected today by a vote of Unionist Party MPs, was to be Brian Faulkner, a former member of Chichester-Clark's cabinet whose past competence was highly regarded.

So, Farewell Then.....

This month saw two notable departures from the world stage - one dictated by mortality, the other a voluntary decision. March 8 was the day that Harold Lloyd, the legendary silent movie actor and comedian, died. Aged 78,
he was considered by many to be at least the equal of - if not superior to
- Charlie Chaplin. *(See Came & Went pages)*
March 16 saw British heavyweight hero Henry Cooper announce his retirement. His move followed a controversial points defeat in London at the fists of a young Joe Bugner and the loss of his British, European and Commonwealth crowns.
(See Sports pages for a full appreciation)

Calley Convicted Of My Lai Massacre Murders

AS REPRESENTATIVES OF THE world news media waited impatiently outside the court-room at Fort Benning, Georgia today, they knew that whatever the decision of the court martial being held inside, it would make front page news. It did.

After 13 days of deliberation, the six officers who had heard four months of evidence against Lt William Calley (pictured), his commanding officer Captain Ernest Medina, and a number of junior rank soldiers, announced that Calley had been found guilty on three of the four counts of murder against him. He had killed 20 Vietnamese civilians in the village of My Lai, in 1968, a case the US Army had managed to hush up until a New York Times journalist, Seymour Hersh, broke it in 1969.

Calley had originally been charged with killing 109 of My Lai's 567 inhabitants - men, women and children - while leading a patrol on a sweep for Viet Cong fugitives. The court had reduced the number of people Calley was found to have massacred in the first two charges, while the fourth charge had been reduced to assault with intent to kill. More importantly, they had completely rejected his attempt to pass responsibility for the slaughter to Capt Medina, who was acquitted of the charges he faced, while charges against 19 members of Calley's unit were also dropped.

Within days of Calley's conviction, and while the court decided whether he should face a death sentence or life imprisonment - the only two sentences available - President Richard Nixon ordered his release on parole until a final judgement was made.

Calley would receive a life sentence, punishment which would be substantially reduced after a series of appeals. He did not get off scot free. But he did get away with murder.

REAL-LIFE DRAMA, NOSTALGIA AND ULTRA-VIOLENCE IN OSCARS BATTLE

A sign of just how much Hollywood's ability to tackle realism had come on in the past few years, *The French Connection* not only confronted the scuzzy underbelly of modern American life head-on, the naturalistic directorial style of William Friedkin added a cinema verité feel to the film's grainy and gripping story and veracity to the warts-and-all performance of Gene Hackman as the New York vice cop bent on busting a heroin gang.

In competition with Stanley Kubrick's stylish working of Anthony Burgess's ultra-violent *A Clockwork Orange*, Peter Bogdanovich's nostalgic small-town tale *The Last Picture Show* and Norman Jewison's vivacious musical *Fiddler On The Roof*, the 1971 Oscars Best Picture shortlist was only tainted by the inclusion of *Nicholas and Alexandra*, the inevitable big-budget stiff its studio forced into a nomination to save some senior executive's face, immense salary and stretch limo.

Although not nominated in the production or direction categories, the likes of *Klute*, *The Go-Between* and *Kotch* were contenders which proved that 1971 had been a pretty good year for cinemagoers.

Major honours (Best Picture, Director and Best Actor) went to *The French Connection*, with Topol (*Fiddler*), Peter Finch (*Sunday, Bloody Sunday*), Walter Matthau (*Kotch*) and George C Scott (*The Hospital*) losing out to Hackman.

The leading lady prize went, deservedly, to Jane Fonda for *Klute*, so edging out rivals Julie Christie (with *McCabe and Mrs Miller*), Glenda Jackson (*Sunday, Bloody Sunday*), Vanessa Redgrave (*Mary, Queen of Scots*) and Janet Suzman (for the only decent performance in *Nicholas and Alexandra*).

Conspiracy theorists suggested that Fonda's Oscar was only won because all the others were British, but that was both unkind and probably inspired by her anti-Vietnam politics.

Represented twice in the Supporting Actor and Supporting Actress stakes (with Jeff Bridges and Ben Johnson, Ellen Burstyn and Cloris Leachman), *The Last Picture Show* team won their only two awards when Johnson and Leachman's names duly came out of the envelopes.

Fiddler On The Roof scored three wins (cinematography, sound and adapted score), while The French Connection's roll continued with an adapted screenplay Oscar for Ernest Tidyman, and another for Jerry Greenberg's superb editing.

A moment of history came with the Original Song Oscar for Shaft to Isaac Hayes, the first African-American to win a music award.

But the greatest moments came when the Academy of Motion Pictures Arts and Sciences membership stood to give Sir Charles Chaplin a five-minute ovation and an Honorary Oscar for a lifetime of achievement. In that audience were many who had been too frightened to defend the comic genius when the McCarthy witch-hunt drove him from America almost 30 years earlier, accused of anti-US tendencies.

'The French Connection' featuring the warts-and-all performance of Gene Hackman as the New York vice cop bent on busting a heroin gang.

APRIL

APRIL 10

IRA Split As Hard-Line Provisionals Break Away

RECENT REPORTS OF AN increasing gulf in the Irish Republican movement were substantially proved correct today in Belfast when the two main wings of the IRA - the 'official' element and the hard-line 'Provisionals' - staged separate marches to commemorate the Easter Rising of 1916 in Dublin.

First to march to the city's Roman Catholic Milltown Cemetery were the 7,000 who'd elected to take part in the Provisionals' remembrance event. They were followed an hour later by only 3,500 supporters of the 'official' IRA parade.

Leaders of both factions were said to have met earlier to set timetables which would ensure there were no open street clashes between rival groups. While British security chiefs were relieved that this arrangement had been negotiated, they were known to be disturbed by the bigger turn-out achieved by the Provisionals, believed to be responsible for the more militant and increasingly violent campaign being waged against British forces based in Ulster. That campaign was taken across the Atlantic for the first time this month when, on April 20, the IRA claimed responsibility for the explosion which sank a Royal Navy launch in Baltimore Harbour during an official visit by a British battleship.

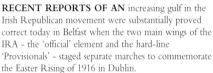

APRIL 6

Revolutionary Stravinsky Composes His Last

Igor Stravinsky, the Russian-born composer who transformed the course of modern classical music with his dramatic and powerful compositions, died in New York today. He was 88 years old.

A student of the great Rimsky-Korsakov, Stravinsky's most outstanding achievements were the scores he wrote for the ballet, The Firebird and Petrushka becoming acclaimed masterpieces when staged by the impressario Diaghilev in Paris, and danced by the legendary Nijinsky. His 1913 opus The Rite of Spring was vilified by critics unable to cope with Stravinsky's use of bold, disrupted rhythms and great slabs of clashing chords, but it gave inspiration to a generation of young composers looking for a new direction.

Stravinsky wrote more great ballet scores in his lifetime than anyone since Tchaikovsky, whom he'd met once in his childhood. During the 1950s his experiments with the 'serial techniques' first explored by Schoenberg led to the creation, among others, of his 1954 work In Memoriam Dylan Thomas, his tribute to the Welsh poet.

After a Russian Orthodox funeral service in New York, Stravinsky's body would be flown to Venice for burial on the island of San Michele.

Hot Pants At Royal Ascot?

The biggest fashion talking point since the mini-skirt hit the streets of London in the Swinging Sixties, Hot pants became the centre of controversy this month when some bright spark had the idea of asking whether women wearing the revealing items would be allowed into the highly select and ultra-decorous Royal Enclosure during this year's Ascot race meetings.

  After huffing, puffing (and probably demolishing a few stiff gins in the process), Ascot management committee members came up with a classic compromise decision. Lest they be considered fuddy-duddy, they said 'yes'. But, just in case that was thought too daring, they added a cautious proviso: only if the 'general effect' was satisfactory.

  No, we don't know what criteria you'd apply to decide that, either!

UK TOP 10 SINGLES

1: Hot Love
- T Rex

2: Bridget The Midget (The Queen Of The Blues)
- Ray Stevens

3: Rose Garden
- Lynn Anderson

4: Jack In The Box
- Clodagh Rodgers

5: There Goes My Everything
- Elvis Presley

6: Walkin'
- CCS

7: Another Day
- Paul McCartney

8: If Not For You
- Olivia Newton-John

9: Power To The People
- John Lennon

10: Love Story (Where Do I Begin)
- Andy Williams

Thousands Killed As Khan Smashes Bangladesh

THOUSANDS OF CIVILIANS were reported to be among those killed by West Pakistan forces which smashed their way through the newly-created independent state of Bangladesh this month in a bid to obliterate the 'Liberation Army' which remained loyal to the rebel government of Sheik Mujibur Rahman. He and his cabinet were said to have abandoned the provisional provincial capital of Chaudanga today as the troops of West Pakistan's President, Yahya Khan, over-ran the city unopposed.

As countless thousands of Bangladeshis began a mass escape to the relative safety of India, it became clear that the West Pakistan army were making absolutely no distinction between Bangladeshi civilians and Liberation Army fighters. More than 7,000 were known to have died in two days and nights of indiscriminate shelling of the capital, Dhaka - among them university students whose still-burning bodies were found in dormitory beds following tank fire into the campus.

The rest of the city fared no better. Army trucks and armoured cars patrolled streets empty except for packs of dogs feeding off the bodies of those caught in the crossfire of battle.

Distressed by the world's apparent indifference to his country's destruction, a provincial assembly member, Muhammed Eunus Ali, was reported as asking foreign journalists: 'Why do you do nothing to help us? The outside world says this is an internal affair. How can you say that when there are thousands of people being killed? This is not an internal affair - this is a pogrom!'

APRIL 21

Haiti's Papa Doc Dies, Baby Doc Takes Over

A momentous day in the troubled history of Haiti, the impoverished Caribbean island state, when its inhabitants learned of the death of François Duvalier, President of Haiti since 1957, when his election was greeted by undisguised delight.

Fondly nicknamed 'Papa Doc' by the people he'd sworn to release from years of corrupt and brutal regimes, Duvalier soon proved himself worse than any who'd held power before him. Using a bizarre but effective blend of wholescale graft, black magic voodoo and the horrific brutality of his private army, the tontons macoutes, Papa Doc became supreme ruler of Haiti, proclaiming himself President for life in 1964.

Any relief that the people of Haiti may have had that the 61 year old Duvalier's life was over, was tempered by the knowledge that his place was to be taken by his 19 year old son and heir, Jean-Claude (pictured) . Known as Baby Doc, his arrival promised no change at all.

APRIL 15

Barbican To Change Shape Of London Skyline

The City of London Council today announced a major development destined to change the ever-shifting shape of London's skyline, when they approved plans for a £17 million ($40m) arts centre as part of the already-started Barbican project.

When completed, The Barbican - a huge complex of shops and flats designed around a man-made lake - will stand in the heart of London's financial centre, adjoining the Moorgate rail station, but with a Tube station of its own.

Although the decision to add the arts centre - which will include concert and theatre spaces, exhibition spaces and restaurants - was widely applauded, critics of the project were keen to remind City authorities that the Barbican was already two years behind schedule.

APRIL 7

Nixon Promises Pull-Out Of Vietnam

America's growing army of anti-war protestors began to sniff the scent of something like victory today when President Nixon committed his administration to an end to US involvement in Vietnam.

Speaking to the nation in a television speech from the Oval Office of the White House, the President said that the US pull-out would begin gradually, but that 100,000 troops would be back home by December.

Nixon's promise - like so many - would prove to be worthless, however.

St Tropez Stampede As Mick Marries Bianca

AMID CHAOTIC SCENES as wild as any he'd experienced in his already eventful and incident-packed life, Rolling Stones singer Mick Jagger took the biggest plunge of that life today in the French Riviera resort of St Tropez when he he exchanged marriage vows with Bianca Pérez Morena de Macias, the Nicaraguan model and socialite he'd met in Paris in September last year.

Camped around the town hall was a small army of reporters, photographers and TV crews, all fighting for a glimpse, or a word, from the wedding guests, including Paul McCartney, Ringo Starr, Eric Clapton, film director Roger Vadim, actress Nathalie Delon and photographer Lord Patrick Lichfield.

Behind the scenes of this fairy-tale wedding, last-minute hitches in details of Mick and Bianca's pre-nuptial contract - no mere nicety in France where the possibility of a separation or divorce has to be viewed objectively - delayed things for an hour.

After a two-week honeymoon in Venice and New York, the couple returned to Paris, where the new Mrs Jagger stayed while her hubby travelled to Keith Richard's house in Villefranche-sur-Mer to begin work on a new Rolling Stones album. Mick and Bianca would become parents on October 21, when their daughter Jade was born.

You do the maths.

Millions Flee Pakistan Holocaust

According to the most reliable figures available today in what had become one of the greatest mass migrations since the end of WWII in Europe, at least two million refugees were said to have fled from the East Pakistan civil war in the past month. Indian medical workers and relief agencies were reported to be struggling to cope, their task made more urgent as impending monsoon rains threatened to flood the border region, bringing the risk of cholera with them.

While the Indian government and international organizations like the Red Cross and Oxfam began appeals and airlifts of supplies to the area, food was in desperately short supply. People waited for hours for tiny portions of rice, with sparse amounts of fresh milk reserved for a few lucky children.

A doctor at one camp asked journalists to send word back to their readers. 'They don't even have straw huts for shelter', he pointed out. Referring to the possibility of a cholera outbreak, he added: 'It's doubtful that we could control an epidemic under these conditions. They will die like flies.'

Arizona Welcomes London Bridge

With due razzamatazz, fireworks and fanfares, the citizens of Arizona this month greeted the official opening of....London Bridge.

Sold, amid a storm of controversy, to a group of Arizona businessmen three years ago when London planners decide to replace the centuries-old original with a concrete and steel marvel capable of carrying modern traffic, the bricks of London Bridge had been numbered, packed and transported to the middle of the Arizona desert, and re-assembled as one of the world's most unusual tourist attractions. Despite all the jokes which tickled British audiences at the time, no-one involved in the US end of the deal thought they were buying Tower Bridge, the one with the road that goes up and down to let tall ships through.

UK TOP 10 SINGLES

1: Knock Three Times
- Dawn
2: Brown Sugar
- The Rolling Stones
3: Double Barrel
- Dave & Ansel Collins
4: It Don't Come Easy
- Ringo Starr
5: Mozart Symphony No 4 In G Minor
- Waldo De Los Rios
6: Indiana Wants Me
- R Dean Taylor
7: Remember Me
- Diana Ross
8: Hot Love
- T Rex
9: Jig A Jig
- East Of Eden
10: Love Story (Where Do I Begin)
- Andy Williams

ARRIVALS

Born this month:
9: Daniela Silvas, Romanian gymnast, former world champion
17: Jordan Knight, US singer, dancer (New Kids On The Block)

DEPARTURES

Died this month:
15: 'Goose' Goslin (Leon Allen Goslin), US baseball star (Washington Senators 1921-1938)
19: Frederick Ogden Nash, US poet, humourist
31: Manuel Ortiz, US bantamweight boxer, world champion 1942-1947, 1947-1950

MAY 16

Sadat Purges Opponents After Foiling Coup

THE STREETS OF CAIRO filled with crowds of cheering Egyptians today as President Anwar Sadat broadcast news that he had foiled an attempted coup and ordered the arrest of a number of aides implicated in the plot. These included his Vice-President, Ali Sabry, a number of cabinet ministers and senior intelligence officers. As the President's supporters called for those involved to be executed for conspiracy and treason, it became clear that the roots of the bid to overthrow Sadat lay in his plan for a political solution to Egypt's long and costly conflict with Israel.

While the President used the failed coup to consolidate his power base - and his aim of negotiated peace with Israel - it was learned that those arrested included Interior Minister Sharawy Gomaa, the War Minister, General Mohammad Fawiz, and the two heads of Egyptian Intelligence. Sadat proved that he would continue to keep faith with Egypt's most valued non-Arab allies on May 28, however, when he signed a new 15-year friendship treaty with the USSR.

MAY 2

Washington Under Siege

President Nixon ordered state police and National Guardsmen into the heart of Washington DC today as more than 30,000 anti-war protestors ignored his calls to quit the campsite they'd created within view of the White House, on the banks of the Potomac River. The demonstration, the biggest to be staged in the US capital since the civil rights march led by Rev Dr Martin Luther King in the 1960s, proved that President Nixon's promise to begin a US pull-out of Vietnam before year end, was not one the peace movement was prepared to accept at face value.

MAY 3

Honecker Becomes East German Leader

Erich Honecher, the 59 year old former German Communist Youth Movement organizer arrested and imprisoned by the Nazis in 1937, and not freed until the arrival of the Russians in 1945, today became the First Secretary of the East German Communist Party, and so effectively head of state.

A member of the Party since 1929, he repeated his pre-war feat of building up the East German Youth Movement between 1949-1958, was promoted to the central committee of the ruling Socialist Unity Party and became principal deputy for Walter Ulbricht, the man whose resignation left the way clear for Honecher's appointment today.

MAY 21

Pompidou Clears British Market Membership

French President Georges Pompidou and British Prime Minister Edward Heath ended two days of talks in Paris today to try to settle the last few outstanding points likely to block Britain's application to become a member of the European Common Market.

According to the most reliable sources, President Pompidou - unlike his predecessor, Charles de Gaulle, who consistently vetoed British approaches for close on 10 years - had decided the road was clear for the current six-strong membership to be increased to ten. Ireland, Denmark and Norway are also expected to have their applications accepted next month.

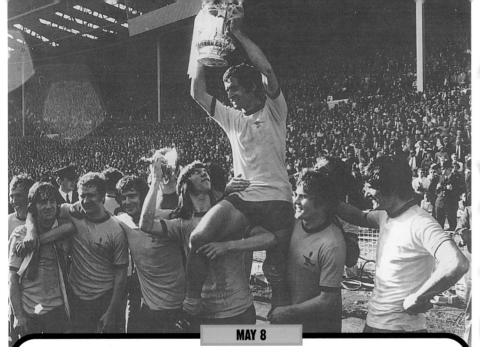

MAY

FA Cup And League Double For Arsenal

Wembley Stadium erupted into a mass of red and white this afternoon as supporters of Arsenal, the north London soccer giants, began celebrating the 20-yard shot on goal by striker Charlie George which won Arsenal the FA Cup - and meant their heroes had finally succeeded in becoming only the second team this century to achieve the double of League and Cup Championships. Their triumph was made especially sweet because the other double had been that of Arsenal's arch-rivals, Tottenham Hotspur, in 1961. And it had been a 1-0 win over Tottenham last week which had given Arsenal a single point victory in the League over Leeds United. Today's scrappy game against Liverpool was no classic, but that George goal nine minutes from the end of extra time gave Arsenal a 2-1 victory, and a darned fine excuse for a really big party.

Councils Attack

Britain's local authorities combined in an attack on Mrs Margaret Thatcher (pictured), the Education Secretary, today, condemning her recent decision to forbid them supplying free milk to schoolchildren. Mrs Thatcher's controversial ruling, which ended the practice of authorities funding milk supplies with money raised in local rates, had led to an immediate outcry - and a vociferous campaign by left-wing groups.

Their tagging of the Education Secretary 'Margaret Thatcher, Milk Snatcher' was taken up by the official parliamentary opposition, and T-shirt manufacturers quick to spot a hot new item.

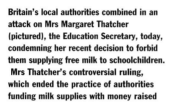

US Newspapers Win 'Pentagon Papers' Verdict

Two leading American newspapers, *The Washington Post* and *The New York Times*, won an historic victory in the US Supreme Court today when a majority of the nine-strong judges panel ruled that the First Amendment of the American Constitution gave them the freedom to print extracts from previously secret documents - the so-called *Pentagon Papers* - on the Vietnam War.

The two papers had published long extracts from a leaked government study of the war's origins and continuing US policy, a move which led to a prosecution by the Justice Department which claimed that publication had jeopardized national security, could harm nuclear arms negotiations and may have delayed the end of the Vietnam War.

The Supreme Court judgement, written by Mr Justice Stewart, reminded the executive that the First Amendment not only guaranteed freedom of the press, but also forbade restraint prior to publication. One of the dissenting minority was Warren Burger, the new Chief Justice appointed by President Nixon.

Common Market Agrees Terms For UK Membership

A YEAR OF HARD bargaining ended today when the British government's chief negotiator, MP Geoffrey Rippon, told a packed House of Commons: 'The back of the negotiations is broken. We have a very satisfactory deal.' Britain was to become a member of the European Economic Community - the Common Market.

Greeted with wild cheers from pro-Marketeers and loud moans from those on both sides of the House who believed membership was A Very Bad Thing, Mr Rippon's announcement ignored the fact that there still remained a lot of haggling before the final terms were agreed. In essence, though, there was agreement that Britain could join the EEC with a place equal to that of founder members France, Italy and Germany.

Heading off anticipated questions on questions uppermost in the minds of anti-Marketeers, Mr Rippon claimed that plans for a transitional period would safeguard the interests of British farmers and fishermen, and the New Zealand dairy industry.

The cost of membership would be around £100 million ($250m) in 1973, rising to £200 million ($500m) by 1977. Responding to complaints that these amounts were higher than expected, Mr Rippon told MPs: 'It is fair and right that we should pay our proper part.'

While France had raised fewer objections to British membership since President de Gaulle's death, it was widely accepted that uneasiness still existed in Paris. That was nothing new and was unlikely to change, ever. As the French themselves say: Plus ça change, plus la même chose - the more things change, the more they stay the same.

UK TOP 10 SINGLES

1: Knock Three Times
- Dawn

2: I Did What I Did For Maria
- Tony Christie

3: Heaven Must Have Sent You
- The Elgins

4: I'm Gonna Run Away From You
- Tami Lynn

5: I Am...I Said
- Neil Diamond

6: Indiana Wants Me
- R Dean Taylor

7: Lady Rose
- Mungo Jerry

8: Banner Man
- Blue Mink

9: My Brother Jake
- Free

10: Chirpy Chirpy Cheep Cheep
- Middle Of The Road

Gandhi Closes Border As Cholera Strikes

Mrs Indira Gandhi, the Indian Prime Minister, ordered troops to seal off her country's border with Bangladesh today, as the unending flood of refugees from the Pakistani civil war was reported hit by an outbreak of cholera.

With Indian and international aid resources stretched past breaking point, Mrs Gandhi was trying to regain some control over a situation which had begun to threaten her government's ability to administer the border area.

UK Shipbuilders Hit By 'Lame Duck' Policy

Upper Clyde Shipbuilders, once one of Britain's most successful marine engineering companies and only source of employment for thousands of Glasgow workers, fell victim to the government's 'lame duck' policy today when a vital rescue package was rejected, forcing the company into liquidation.

The decision, confirmed in the House of Commons by John Davies, the Trade and Industry Secretary, came in for a vitriolic attack from Labour's former Technology Minister, Anthony Wedgwood Benn, who once injected £20 million ($50m) of public funds into Upper Clyde.

Ironically, it was Mr Benn who coined the phrase 'lame duck' as part of his policy concerning industry rescues. The government had borrowed it to justify their refusal to prop up what they considered to be lost causes.

Ali Clears His Name

Former world heavyweight boxing champ Muhammad Ali won his four-year fight to clear himself from charges of being a draft dodger today when the US Supreme Court ruled that his refusal to serve in Vietnam on religious and moral grounds should have been accepted by the authorities, and should not have caused the boxing world to strip him of his title and effectively stop his brilliant career.

Ali, who dropped his given name of Cassius Clay when he became a Muslim in 1964, had managed to return to the ring in 1970, when he lost a title bid against Joe Frazier on points. But it was, perhaps, more important to the 29 year old that the slur of his name - with its implications of cowardice - should be lifted.

Cosmonauts Found Dead In Russian Spacecraft

THREE SOVIET COSMONAUTS - Vladislav Volkov, Georgi Dubrovolsky and Victor Passayev - were found dead in their *Soyuz 11* spacecraft after an apparently routine flight and landing. Confirming their mysterious deaths, the Tass news agency could throw no light on the tragedy, but did confirm that an intensive inquiry had been ordered.

The three men took off on their trip on June 6. During what had previously been hailed as a triumphant exercise, they had established a new space endurance record by remaining in orbit for more than three weeks.

Linking with a *Salyut* space laboratory, the cosmonauts had returned to *Soyuz 11* just before making what appeared to be an absolutely textbook descent to earth. When the recovery team reached them, however, they were all dead. Among the first expressions of regret at the Soviet tragedy was a message of condolence from members of the US NASA team in Houston, always rivals but also brothers in spirit.

The streets of Moscow would be filled with thousands of mourning citizens on July 2, when the three space heroes were given a full state funeral.

Fairfield shipyard

SPORT

THREE-IN-A-ROW OPEN WINS PUT TREVINO IN RECORD BOOKS

Always one of the most popular players on the championship golf circuit, Texan-born Lee Trevino secured his place in the record books this year with an unprecedented three Open wins - the US, the Canadian and the British - in as many weeks.

Talking up a storm, the man who'd been raised in a Dallas shack without running water or electricity, and left school at the age of 14, stormed his way around the Merion, Pennsylvania, course to earn a play-off against Jack Nicklaus, during which the joker threw a rubber snake towards his opponent. Trevino's three-stroke win owed nothing to that ill-considered prank - Nicklaus was simply outplayed.

A matter of days later, Trevino also found himself in a play-off in Montreal after catching Art Wall with three late birdies. Unlike the full 18-hole US decider, the Canadian Open had a sudden-death policy and a first-hole birdie was enough to give Trevino the title.

A week later, the 32 year old gradually overcame the first and second round challenges of Tony Jacklin, Howie Johnston, Vicente Fernandez and Liang Huan Lu to face a third-day battle with Jacklin and Lu. Beginning with the luxury of a three-stroke lead, Trevino managed to make his third successive Open victory a tight-run thing when he fell foul of Birkdale's treacherous and precipitous dunes on the 71st hole.

Even with a double-bogey seven, Trevino managed to beat the Formosan by one stroke when Lu failed to get the last-hole birdie four he needed to force a play-off.

Typically, Trevino had a one-liner handy for journalists who asked him about the pressures of that last-minute victory. 'You don't know what pressure is', Trevino said, 'until you play for five bucks with two bucks in your pocket!'

COOPER QUITS AFTER BUGNER 'STEALS' TITLES

Already a national hero, thanks to his 1963 fourth round flooring of the young Cassius Clay - who was only saved from a shock defeat by the bell - Henry Cooper's loss of his British, Commonwealth and European heavyweight titles to Joe Bugner on March 16 this year remains one of the most disputed decisions ever witnessed in a British boxing ring.

It would have long-term ramifications for Cooper. Outraged at the verdict, he announced his retirement from the sport, leaving a gap no other British heavyweight could fill, either in skill or popularity, until the emergence of Frank Bruno in 1982.

Fittingly, Bruno's ascendancy would be at the expense of an over-the-hill Bugner, so ensuring the thanks and loyalty of fight fans still outraged at the latter's victory this year.

JACKIE STEWART REGAINS CROWN WITH SIX WINS

Completely overshadowed in 1970 by the runaway dominance of Jochen Rindt, who won the world motor racing championship despite his death in practice for the Italian Grand Prix, Scotland's Jackie Stewart took the 1971 Grand Prix season by the scruff of the neck to register six emphatic wins and – with team-mate François Cevert always close behind – help Tyrrell storm away with the constructors' title.

Stewart's victories were in the Spanish, Monaco, French, British, German and Canadian events, while Cevert won the US and came second to Stewart in France and Germany.

Between them, Stewart and Cevert accounted for seven of the season's 11 races - as emphatic a championship run as could be imagined.

Henry Cooper and Joe Bugner at the weigh-in for their Wembley fight

LEEDS AND CHELSEA WIN EUROPEAN TITLES

English teams proved themselves championship material in two key European tournaments this season, though neither found victory easy.

In the last Fairs Cup (it would be re-named the UEFA Cup in 1972), Leeds United had to face the mighty Juventus over two hard-fought legs. In Turin, honours were shared as Madeley and Bates replied to Bettega and Capello's goals for Juventus. It was tight in Leeds too,

with the second leg finishing 1-1, Alan Clark and Anastasi having the pleasure of seeing their names on the score sheet. On the away-goals rule, it was Leeds who had their names added to the trophy's roll of honour.

The European Cup Winners Cup final between Real Madrid and Chelsea also went to two games when the first meeting in Athens ended 1-1. On that occasion, Osgood and Zoco were the scorers.

In the replay, also in Athens, Chelsea emerged champions when Fleitas was the only Real player able to answer the Chelsea goals of Dempsey and Osgood.

Mystery Death Of Rock Bad-Boy Morrison

CREATING AS MUCH controversy and confusion in death as he ever did in his stormy 28 years of life, the body of American rock star Jim Morrison was reported to have been found in the bath of his Paris apartment today, apparently victim of a major heart attack.

Founder, principal songwriter and lead singer of The Doors, Morrison (pictured) had quit the group earlier in the year, saying he wanted to concentrate on writing, and possibly recording, the poetry he wanted to be his real and lasting contribution to posterity. He was also under pressure from the stress of preparing his appeal against a conviction for exposing himself on stage during a Doors concert in Miami in 1969.

A film student at UCLA before forming The Doors in 1965, Morrison's readiness to shock and outrage in the name of art led to him tackling the subject of incest and family murder in his song *The End,* while his increased use

of and dependency on alcohol and drugs led to establishment outrage.

Mystery surrounding Morrison's death led to speculation that the coffin which was buried in the Père Lachaise cemetery in Paris (also resting place of Oscar Wilde and Edith Piaf) was empty, with a still-living star enjoying the bliss of an anonymous hermit existence.

It was the stuff of legend, and that legend continues to this day, with his Paris resting place still the site of fan pilgrimages, vigils, floral tributes and loving graffiti the Père Lachaise staff are forced to tidy up constantly.

Rescue Drama As Sub Sinks

There was high drama today in Portsmouth Harbour, the south coast port which is principal home to Britain's Royal Navy fleet, when the submarine HMS *Artemis* sank at its moorings, leaving three crewmen trapped inside its flooded hulk. Submarines are supposed to sink, of course, but preferably under controlled conditions. Apparently, someone pushed the wrong button and opened sea-cocks which allowed the waters of the River Solent to flood in. Not the right way to do it. A desperate rescue mission dominated news media for more than 36 hours before the three men were thankfully saved from the airtight compartment which had almost proved to be their tomb.

Barnard Makes First Heart And Lung Transplant

Four years after he became the first surgeon to carry out a successful human heart transplant operation, South African specialist Dr Christiaan Barnard was today reported as having succeeded in performing the world's first heart and lungs transfer, at Cape Town's Groote Schuur Hospital.
With many surgeons still experiencing long-term problems with tissue rejection, and the number of ordinary transplants having reduced while attempts were made to eliminate, or substantially reduce, the risk to recipient patients, Dr Barnard's achievement was questioned by a number of other eminent surgeons.

One such was Donald Ross, a consultant at London's National Heart Hospital. While he said he'd be delighted to be proved wrong, he said he knew of no medical development that could justify Dr Barnard's return to transplant work, even if the combined transplant was important.

UK TOP 10 SINGLES

1: Chirpy Chirpy Cheep Cheep
- Middle Of The Road

2: Co-Co
- Sweet

3: Don't Let It Die
- Hurricane Smith

4: Banner Man
- Blue Mink

5: Me And You And A Dog Named Boo
- Lobo

6: Get It On
- T Rex

7: Black And White
- Greyhound

8: He's Gonna Step On You Again
- John Kongos

9: Just My Imagination (Running Away With Me)
- The Temptations

10: Monkey Spanner
- Dave & Ansel Collins

Born this month:
9: Kelvin Grant, UK
pop/reggae singer
(Musical Youth)

DEPARTURES
Died this month:
1: Sir Learie Constantine,
Trinidadian and West
Indian batsman, lawyer,
civil rights activist; High
Commissioner of Trinidad
and Tobago 1962-1964
(see Came & Went pages)
3: Jim Morrison, US rock
singer, writer (The Doors)
(see main story)
6: Daniel Louis
Armstrong, US jazz
pioneer

JULY 31

US Astronauts Go Driving On The Moon

SCIENCE FICTION BECAME science fact today when US astronauts James Irwin and David Scott wheeled what was officially called a Lunar Roving Vehicle, but which commentators immediately labelled *The Moon Buggy*, and drove it several miles through the rock-strewn landscape of the moon.

The seventh and eighth men to walk on the surface, but the first to venture out under power, Irwin and Scott had landed *Falcon,* the lunar module of their *Apollo 15* spacecraft, in the Sea of Rains the day before. Their partner, Alfred Worden, remained aboard their mother ship in lunar orbit.

Although they encountered problems with the buggy's front-wheel steering the astronauts were able to negotiate their way by using the independent rear-wheel controls. With a communications aerial mounted on the machine, Irwin and Scott were able to film themselves collecting rock samples from the rim of Elbow Crater and send magnificent colour TV images back to NASA flight control in Houston.

The two would make further successful trips in the buggy before returning to *Apollo 15* and a safe splashdown in the Pacific on August 7, to be true makers of history.

JULY 2

Wimbledon Upset As Goolagong Beats Court

Reigning champion Margaret Court's defence of her Wimbledon women's singles title was never going to be the formality her fans predicted. With American ace Billie-Jean King itching to regain the crown she'd lost to Britain's Ann Jones in 1969, and the likes of Rosie Casals and Virginia Wade also waiting to block her way, the Australian Grand Slam diva always faced tough competition.

As it happened, none of those mentioned featured the shock-horror headlines which followed Court's surprise defeat today. They belonged to a largely unknown and completely unfancied Australian newcomer, 19 year old Evonne Goolagong (pictured), who stunned Court and the Centre Court crowd with a staggering 6-4, 6-1 demolition of her long-time idol.

Coming to Wimbledon with the French clay-court title recently won, the part-aboriginal Goolagong rang warning bells when she beat Billie-Jean King in the semis with a mixture of grace and power which thrilled the Wimbledon thousands, and the millions watching on TV around the world.

Riviera Police Eject Topless Sunbathers

The unimaginable happened on the French Riviera today - riot police invaded beaches to evict topless (female) sunbathers who refused to obey a recent local edict banning such wanton displays.

Famous resorts which once epitomized France's world reputation for a healthy, relaxed, open attitude to all things sensual - including St Tropez, home of Brigitte Bardot, one-time one-woman marketing campaign for the pleasures of letting it all hang out - had decided that times and attitudes had somehow changed, and such behaviour was now unseemly!

Jordan Attacks Last PLO Bases

King Hussein of Jordan today ordered his army to mount a series of massive attacks on the last known surviving bases of the Palestine Liberation Organization (PLO) left on Jordanian soil.

The exercise finally ended what the King had begun last September when, following PLO attempts to overthrow him, he had negotiated a peace settlement which - while it gave Jordan the responsibility of protecting Palestinian refugee camps - also meant that PLO guerrillas must leave the country. While most PLO forces had followed their leader, Yasir Arafat, to new bases in Syria, Lebanon and Libya, some remained to be persuaded to join them. With force, if necessary.

35

Ulster Explodes After Internment Round-Up

TWELVE PEOPLE WERE KILLED and many injured - one of them a priest adminstering the last rites to a dying man, another a 15 year old boy shot by soldiers as he attempted to throw a petrol bomb - as the IRA reacted savagely to the round-up and arrest of more than 300 suspected terrorists this week under new emergency powers introduced by the British government.

The suspects faced internment without trial as investigations began into their alleged links with paramilitary groups, a move the Irish Prime Minister Jack Lynch described as 'deplorable evidence of the political poverty' of Britain's Ulster policies, and led the shadow Home Secretary, James Callaghan, to call for a Council of All-Ireland to help resolve the conflict.

In a further attempt to defuse tension in Ulster, the government banned all provocative processions, including the Orange Day parades held annually by Protestants and the Apprentice Boys march mounted by Catholics in Londonderry. The only exception would be Remembrance Day ceremonies to honour the dead of the two world wars.

Ulster's new Prime Minister, Brian Faulkner, described the paramilitary organizations on both sides of the divide as 'those who have murdered in cold blood, created situations which have led to death or injury to people quite uninvolved in disorder, maimed numerous people, including young children, and put at risk their jobs and the whole future of their entire communities.'

Charging police with brutality against those interned and interrogated on board a British Navy ship moored in Londonderry and at local prisons, the IRA used a bomb to destroy the gates of Belfast's Crumlin Road Jail on August 22.

Heath Ignores Crisis To Win Admiral Cup

With his administration embroiled in the most serious challenge yet to its authority in Ulster, British Prime Minister Edward Heath today decided to accept a challenge of a completely different type, and honour his promise to captain the British team taking part in the gruelling 600-mile Fastnet yacht race, climax to the annual Admiral's Cup all-round test of ocean-racing skills. Although his yacht, *Morning Cloud* (pictured), was the last to enter Plymouth Harbour after losing part of her spinnaker gear off the Isles of Scilly, where Labour leader Harold Wilson had a holiday home (cue *The Twilight Zone* theme?), the British team emerged victors.

Harvey Raises Two Fingers As Appeal Succeeds

British showjumper Harvey Smith raised two fingers in the now-traditional 'V-for-victory' salute today - partly to please eager press photographers, partly to celebrate his successful appeal against being disqualified after winning the British Showjumping Derby, and partly to show the world what he'd really done when the Derby stewards thought he'd done something very different.

Confused? So was Harvey. According to him, he'd raised those two fingers in triumph when he knew he'd won the title two nights earlier at London's Olympia Stadium. The judges believed his hand was turned the other way and those fingers signalled an 'up you' insult, so they'd disqualified him. With the press and public laughingly behind him, Harvey Smith - a long-time scourge of the horsey establishment, got his title back.

AUGUST 18

George Best First Victim Of League's 'Get Tough' Policy

The new English football season began today, with managers and players warned that the Football League had ordered referees to get tough with anyone whose conduct they considered less than ideal, including those who committed so-called 'professional fouls' such as handling the ball, or persistently abused them or questioned their decisions.

To no-one's great surprise, one of the first players to fall foul of the policy and be sent off to enjoy an early bath, was George Best, Manchester United's volatile and wayward genius.

Playing at Stamford Bridge, where his team were beaten 3-2 by Chelsea, Best was given his marching orders for continually arguing with the man in black. He'd been warned.

Rock Stars Unite To Aid Bangladesh

SOME OF THE WORLD'S biggest rock, pop and classical stars suspended their egos in New York tonight and, led by former Beatle George Harrison, joined forces to create a charity fund to aid the millions of people left homeless and starving in the Bangladesh war of independence with Pakistan.

The artists, who included Eric Clapton, Bob Dylan, Ringo Starr, George Harrison and Ravi Shankar (pictured), the classical Indian sitar player who was Harrison's musical guru, played two sell-out concerts at Madison Square Garden, more than 40,000 paying around $250,000 to start the appeal ball rolling.

The evening was filmed and recorded, with a triple LP rush-released worldwide only a few weeks later. With all participants giving their services free and Harrison waiving his royalties from the proceeds, *The Concert For Bangladesh* project would prove that the rock 'n' roll generation had well and truly grown up, and was prepared to do its bit to make things better, when it could.

IRA Plan British Bomb Campaign As Ulster Burns

Belfast was awash with rumour tonight after Joe Cahill, the city's IRA chief, held a surprise news conference to refute British Army claims that the recent internment operation had 'virtually defeated' the hard core of IRA gunmen in Ulster.

Cahill described the claim as mere propaganda. No more than 30 of the 300 or more men being held were active IRA men, he said - 'no more than a pinprick' against the support the IRA really had at their disposal.

The press conference was held amid a further build-up of activity by police and Special Branch surveillance teams. They were concentrating their efforts on British ports after reliable intelligence sources warned that frustrated IRA Provisionals were planning a major bombing campaign on the British mainland.

In Ulster, meanwhile, the fresh terror of organized arson had left 2,000 Protestants and 5,000 Catholics homeless in Belfast. In four nights of attacks, gunmen began forcing their way into houses, ordering the occupants into the street - often in no more than nightwear - and lighting fires with petrol.

Church halls and community centres were commandeered as emergency dormitories for victim families, but many homeless Catholics took trains south, where the Irish government had set up temporary accomodation in camps.

BRITISH GUYS GO GLAM, BUT US SAYS NO

Since The Beatles first bridged the Atlantic, it was very rare for a big British act not to succeed to some extent in the US. This year, however, saw the birth of a trend which would remain an almost exclusively British phenomenon American record-buyers found it all too easy to resist, with a few exceptions. Glam rock was born in 1971.

It arrived with a group called T Rex, led by a striking young singer-songwriter-guitarist called Marc Bolan who wore make-up, and gave off very ambivelant sexual messages. They had four big hits this year - *Ride A White Swan, Hot Love, Get It On and Jeepster* - to set their, and Glam Rock's, ball rolling.

T Rex would become a reasonably successful act in the US, with the 1972 *Bang A Gong (Get It On)* a No 10 high-spot. Bolan would die in a car crash in 1977.

Hot on T Rex's heels came Sweet, a quartet with a stream of hit songs written by Nicky Chinn and Mike Chapman, which began in July with *Co-Co* and would include the likes of *Wig Wag Bam, Blockbuster, Hellraiser* and *Ballroom Blitz* before they ran out of steam in 1975.

With June came *Rock 'n' Roll Part 2*, the first appearance of Gary Glitter, the man who came to epitomize Glam Rock well past its sell-by date. The man born Paul Gadd, but who'd been Paul Russell, Paul Raven and Paul Monday before he and producer Mike Leander went for broke with costumes to match the

newest name, went on to score immense hits with *I Didn't Know I Loved You, Hello Hello I'm Back Again, I'm The Leader Of The Gang* and *I Love You Love* pretty well everywhere - except the United States, apart from a brief appearance by the debut single.

In August, Britain got the first glimpse of Slade, another load of over-the-top dressers, who covered Little Richard's *Get Down Get With It* to test the water, and returned in November with their first No 1, *Coz I Luv You*. Outrageous clothes, outrageous singing from vocalist/foghorn Noddy Holder, and more outrageous spelling as Slade scored with the likes of *Look Wot You Dun, Take Me Bak 'Ome, Cum On Feel The Noize* giving them six No 1 hits and an unbroken five-year chart run with everything they released.

Poking their heads above the parapets for the first time in 1971 were a Scottish band destined to become Britain's biggest teen-appeal band between 1974 and 1976. Unlike the others, The Bay City Rollers would translate UK success into US chart hits in a big way, but for now, their *Keep On Dancing* would prove only a toe in the water. They'd go away with manager Tam Paton to perfect the bizarre mix of tartan and flares which countless thousands of fans would want to copy when the time came.

For now, Glam Rock was just emerging, and things were only just beginning to get deliciously silly.

T-Rex set the Glam ball rolling

42 Killed As Attica State Prison Inmates Revolt

FLAMES AND SMOKE FILLED the air at Attica State Prison, New York, tonight as the most serious inmate uprising in American history reached the end of what would be only the first day of a four-day siege, brought to a bloody end when troops stormed in to recapture the complex. Thirty-two prisoners and 10 warders would be killed.

The revolt began when prisoners managed to overpower guards and seize control of a high-security wing. Although the authorities would succeed in stopping the prisoners from taking over the whole prison, at least 1,000 were able to rampage through the sections they had 'liberated', burning, smashing and destroying large areas. At the height of the riot, 32 warders were held hostage.

An official inquiry team would be set up on September 30 to study the causes of the revolt. The team, which included a former inmate who had served time for drug offences and forgery, would find that a refusal to concede to Black Power prisoners' requests for segregated 'accomodation' had been the main trigger for events at Attica.

SEPTEMBER 9

Hostage Ambassador Released By Guerrillas

A prisoner of left-wing Tupamaros guerrillas for the past eight months, the British Ambassador to Uruguay, Geoffrey Jackson (pictured), found himself a free man once more tonight when his captors let him out of a car on the corner of a street in the Nuevo Paris suburb of the capital, Montevideo.

Taken in by a local priest, Mr Jackson took Communion and offered thanks in the Church of St Francis of Assisi while waiting for British Embassy officials and local police to collect him and take him for a check-up at Montevideo's British hospital. He was reported to be fit and well, although there had been fears for his health because of a heart condition.

Mr Jackson's release came only days after a mass escape of Tupamaros followers from a Montivideo prison. Uruguayan government officials denied suggestions that this may have been 'allowed' as part of a deal to arrange the Ambassador's freedom.

SEPTEMBER 29

Records Tumble As Chelsea Score Baker's Dozen

Having won last season's European Cup-winners' Cup by beating the once-mighty Real Madrid 2-1 in a final replay in Athens, Chelsea FC made another definite mark on the tournament today when they thrashed Luxembourg's Jeunesse Hautcharage 13-0 at Stamford Bridge during the second leg of their second round defence of the title.

As they'd already strolled through to an 8-0 win in Luxembourg, Chelsea established a still-unbeaten and probably unassailable 21-0 aggregate total. While they would not go the distance, the trophy would remain in Britain when Glasgow Rangers beat Moscow Dynamo 3-2 in the Barcelona final.

UK TOP 10 SINGLES

1: Hey Girl Don't Bother Me
- The Tams
2: I'm Still Waiting
- Diana Ross
3: Never Ending Song Of Love
- The New Seekers
4: Did You Ever
- Nancy Sinatra & Lee Hazlewood
5: What Are You Doing Sunday
- Dawn
6: Soldier Blue
- Buffy Sainte-Marie
7: Back Street Luv
- Curved Air
8: Nathan Jones
- The Supremes
9: It's Too Late
- Carole King
10: Let Your Yeah Be Yeah
- The Pioneers

SEPTEMBER 24

Britain Deports 90 Soviet 'Spies'

In an unprecedented move bound to strain British-Soviet relations and lead to 'tit-for-tat' reprisals, 90 Russian diplomats and trade officials were today ordered to leave Britain by the Home Secretary, Sir Alec Douglas-Home, accused of using their jobs as a cover for spying.

Acting on information supplied by a senior KGB defector, Sir Alec said Britain would not tolerate the 'hive of Russian intelligence activity' he claimed existed behind the façades of the USSR's Embassy and Trade Missions in London.

On October 8, the expected Russian retaliation came when five British diplomats were expelled from Moscow, and entry visa applications for 13 other Britons were rejected.

SEPTEMBER 11

Khrushchev, Disgraced Soviet Supremo, Dies

NIKITA KHRUSHCHEV (pictured), the Soviet leader who took the world to the brink of an atomic war during the Cuban missile crisis of 1962, but fell foul of Politburo arch-conservatives who deposed him in 1964, died today in complete obscurity, his passing unmarked and unmourned by the regime which dismantled most of the reforms he introduced. He was 77 years old.

As Soviet Prime Minister from 1958 until his fall, Khrushchev did much to destroy and disgrace the Stalinist system he'd survived by being an obedient clown prince to the tyrant. While his tendency to histrionics - like using his shoe to beat out emphasis to his UN General Assembly tirade threatening to bury the West - was a gift to cartoonists and comedians, foreign statesmen were only too aware of his ability to act with complete ruthlessness.

It was Khrushchev who ordered the Red Army to smash the Hungarian uprising in 1956 and maintained an inflexible grip on the policies of eastern Europe's Communist regimes. It was Khrushchev who decided to face down the US over the question of Soviet missiles in Cuba, and his defeat by President Kennedy in that war of wills started the process which ended in his fall from power.

SEPTEMBER 14

Russian Jazz Fans Salute Duke

A standing ovation and near-hysteria greeted American jazz legend Duke Ellington in Leningrad tonight as he and his orchestra played their first-ever concert behind the Iron Curtain.

His Russian tour, the first by a major US jazz figure, ended long months of negotiations at the highest government levels. Many hard-line elements within the Politburo still considered jazz a decadent music.

Not so the thousands of Russian fans who made the tour a complete sell-out, and who paid small fortunes to buy black market tickets for a first glimpse of the maestro in the flesh.

SEPTEMBER 7

PMs Meet As Ulster Mourns 100th Victim

The death of Annette McGavigan, a 14 year old schoolgirl hit by a high velocity bullet as British troops and IRA snipers exchanged fire in the streets of Londonderry today, added an extra sense of urgency to talks being held between Prime Minister Edward Heath and Jack Lynch, his Irish counterpart. Annette was the 100th victim of the civil war now raging across Ulster.

As the two premiers tried to find a way to defuse the apparently worsening situation and devise a long-term solution acceptable to all sides in the conflict, Annette left her home, telling a friend she wanted to find a rubber bullet for her growing collection of war souvenirs. She was caught in the crossfire which broke out as she set off on her trophy hunt.

The near impossibility of the task facing Heath and Lynch was typified by a speech in Larne by William Craig, a right-wing Unionist leader. Refusing to admit the province's Republican minority would respond to anything but force, he called for the British military presence to be increased to at least 20,000.

SEPTEMBER 28

Hungarian Cardinal Ends Embassy Exile

Cardinal Josef Mindszenty, the 79 year old Roman Catholic Primate of Hungary, ended his 25 years of self-imposed exile inside the US Embassy in Budapest today. After receiving welcome and tributes from still-loyal followers, he flew to Rome and an audience with the Pope.

The Cardinal first sought sanctuary in the Embassy when the 1956 Hungarian uprising was crushed, refusing to leave until charges against him were dropped. He was wise to do so - most of the Hungarian leaders who did surrender to the Soviet puppet regime were killed after secret trials, despite promises of fair treatment. The current Hungarian regime were only too happy for Mindszenty to leave Hungary. As long as he remained, a virtual prisoner, in the Embassy, he remained a potent martyr symbol for Hungarian dissidents.

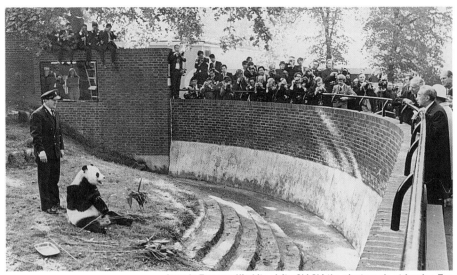

Japan's Emperor Hirohito visits Chi-Chi the giant panda at London Zoo

Londoners Welcome Hirohito With Silence

OCTOBER 9

AS OFFICIAL STATE VISITS GO, today's arrival in London of Japan's Emperor Hirohito was greeted by a distinctly cool response from the crowds who watched his motorcade travel from Heathrow Airport to Buckingham Palace. A quarter of a century may have passed since his nation surrendered to put a final end to the Second World War, but memories of the atrocities committed in his name as Supreme Ruler still survived, and his progress was marked by an often eerie silence.

The national mood was summed up by the Queen who, in her remarkably frank speech of welcome, told Hirohito: 'We cannot pretend that the past did not exist. We cannot pretend that relations between our two peoples have always been peaceful and friendly.'

That was reinforced by calls from organizations representing former prisoners of war brutalized by Japanese captors. They demanded a boycott of Japanese goods and for people to ignore Hirohito's public engagements.

Public Say No, Commons Say Yes To EEC

With all the opinion polls saying that most British people didn't want it, and the Labour Party voting to oppose it, Prime Minister Edward Heath led his Conservative Party faithful through the lobbies of the House of Commons today to win a 356-244 majority approval for his cabinet's decision, in principle, to join the Common Market.

As should only be expected from a move which had so divided public opinion, Mr Heath's victory was not won on straightforward party lines. In fact, 39 Conservative MPs voted against the government, while 69 pro-market Labour rebels voted with the motion in defiance of their recent Party Conference decision, by 5-1, to reject entry on the terms negotiated by the Tories.

Archie's A Foul-Mouthed US Hit

Racing to the top of the US TV ratings this month as the smash hit of the new season, was a character already very well known, admired and loathed by British telly-watchers - only they knew him by a different name.

For close on 10 years the loud-mouthed, foul-mouthed, bigoted, biased and sexist Alf Garnett had been the star of BBC-TV's *'Til Death Do Us Part*. In America, the same character - with the same hang-ups, prejudices and inability to stop sounding off - was re-named Archie Bunker, and the show was re-titled *All In The Family*. Just as Alf Garnett had helped make a star out of actor Warren Mitchell, so Archie Bunker would catapult Carroll O'Connor to the front of news magazines as America's chattering classes wondered whether the show's outstanding success was a sign that Bunker was only saying what the rest of the nation wished it had the nerve to utter aloud. They'd have to keep wondering for eight more years, as *All In The Family* rolled on, and Archie didn't mellow.

Warhol Show Gives Tate A Hit

London's Tate Gallery had a major hit on their hands this month as it opened its doors to record crowds flooding in to catch the major retrospective of works by notorious American artist Andy Warhol. Extra staff had been recruited to cope with expected demand, but even they were overwhelmed by the sheer weight of numbers.

Although it was widely known that Warhol, now pretty well famous for being famous, had long ago ceased to execute most of his works himself, leaving that to teams of helpers in his New York workshop, The Factory, it seemed that thousands of people were prepared to stand in line for hours for a glimpse of his soup cans and multiple photo-images of pop icons like Marilyn Monroe and Jackie Kennedy.

OCTOBER 25

US Humbled As UN Accepts Mao And Ejects Chiang

WHILE A FURIOUS US DELEGATE, George Bush, condemned it as 'a moment of infamy' and Britain's Sir Colin Crowe described it as 'a return to reality', the General Assembly of the United Nations tonight voted to admit Communist China to full membership, and expel the Nationalist Chinese regime of General Chiang Kai-shek.

The UN vote - an Albanian inspired move which took US delegates by surprise, making it impossible for them to stop it taking place - was an overwhelming and humiliating defeat for US plans to allow both Chinese governments to be represented.

Among the 76 nations which supported the Albanian motion to expel the Nationalists, was Britain. While a Tanzanian delegate performed an impromptu victory dance in front of the Assembly, delegation leader Sir Colin Crowe said it was 'the right result.'

President Nixon and Chiang Kai-shek didn't agree. The US leader, while keen to help a Washington-Beijing thaw by relaxing America's 26 year embargo on Mao Tse-tung's repeated applications for a UN seat, had also lobbied hard for the Formosan regime to be allowed to stay on.

In Formosa, the General said the UN had 'bowed to the forces of evil' and vowed to continue his fight to overthrow the Beijing government, which would take its UN seat a month later.

OCTOBER 31

Royal Navy Quits Singapore

Britain's close 151-year relationship with Singapore, the island republic south of the Malayan peninsula, came to a final end today when 17 British warships sailed away from the port to mark the shut-down of the Royal Navy's Far East Command headquarters. A strategically important base for British naval forces in South-East Asia for most of the century, and a full member of the Commonwealth since 1965, Singapore was acquired for the East India Company by Sir Stamford Raffles in 1819. Its capture by Japanese troops in 1942 was described by Winston Churchill as 'the worst disaster and largest capitulation in British history'.

OCTOBER 31

IRA Bomb Blasts London's Post Office Tower

IRA terrorists today proved that they could carry out their threats to bring the Ulster fight to the British mainland when they bombed one of London's most dramatic landmarks, the Post Office Tower, in the early hours of this morning.

The capital's tallest building and a popular tourist attraction, the Tower proved a far too easy target for the terrorists. Their bomb ripped huge holes in the windows of an observation platform under the revolving restaurant, showering glass and debris on streets hundreds of feet below.

The Tower was sealed off, never to re-open as a public venue. And the questions began.Why had security been so lax? Where would the IRA strike next?

Louis Armstrong

JULY 6

LOUIS ARMSTRONG - NOW YOU HAS JAZZ!

No other entertainer or musician epitomized the rise of jazz - from its highly disreputable beginnings in the less than salubrious surroundings of Southern US brothels, gin palaces and bars, to its acceptance as an art form in the world's leading concert halls and theatres - than Louis

'Satchmo' Armstrong, who died today aged 71, thus the same age as this century.

Raised as an orphan in The Colored Waifs Home in New Orleans, Armstrong honed his untutored cornet playing skills in various local dance and marching bands before joining the legendary King Oliver's Creole Jazz Band in 1922. The recordings they made together during the next two years would establish Armstrong as one of the most remarkable new finds in jazz.

Now playing trumpet, the series of recordings he made

with The Fletcher Henderson Orchestra, and then as leader of his own Hot Five and Hot Seven bands, all combined to confirm his supremacy. Work with a wide variety of singers and line-ups through the 1930s and 1940s, including extensive European and British tours which began in the 1930s, helped make him undisputed king of jazz on an international level.

In the 1940s Armstrong began to diversify. Always acknowledged as one of the best singers in jazz, he switched to a role as all-round entertainer, appeared in a number of successful films (most notably *High Society*, with Frank Sinatra and Bing Crosby) and had pop chart hits with songs like *Hello Dolly* and *What A Wonderful World* to end his full and rich life as one of the most popular artists in that world.

MARCH 8
HAROLD LLOYD - SILENT DAREDEVIL SUPERSTAR

For close on 15 years, the name of Harold Lloyd above the title of a film was a solid guarantee of huge box-office success. People everywhere would, it seemed, do anything but miss one of the hundreds of 'shorts' and two-reelers the dapper, solemn, bespectacled comic actor made from 1916 onwards.

The thing which marked Lloyd, who was born in 1893, apart from every comedy star of the time - including his great rival Charlie Chaplin - was his ability to not only come up with the most astonishing cliff-hanging stunts to put audiences on the edge of their seats, but his insistence that he do those stunts himself.

Whether it was hanging from the hands of a clock, clinging to a flagpole high above a busy street, or strolling casually along, apparently unaware of high-speed vehicles missing him by inches, Lloyd was a master at mixing laughs and suspense.

The arrival of sound triggered a decline in his career, but he continued to make films regularly until 1938. Better late than never, he was presented with an Honorary Oscar in 1952, the citation naming him as 'a master comedian and good citizen'.

JULY 1
SIR LEARIE CONSTANTINE - FROM BATSMAN TO STATESMAN

No cricket player ever represented his country with greater aggression, fire, spirit and skill than Learie Constantine - and no man ever came to represent his country in the diplomatic arena with greater dignity and quiet effectiveness.

A complete all-rounder, Constantine could bowl either medium-fast or very fast, and was a quite brilliant fielder. He also hit a ball with a bat harder than anyone, which made his innings a thrill for the thousands who packed grounds to watch him play. For 10 years, in the Lancashire Leagues he helped Nelson to eight league titles.

A law student, Constantine was called to the Bar of London's Middle Temple in 1954 and began a distinguished legal career marked by expertise in politics and race relations. Appointed High Commisioner in Britain for Trinidad and Tobago in 1962, he was knighted in the same year, and created a Life Peer in 1969.

Princess Anne Voted Sportswoman Of The Year

NOVEMBER 5

NOW ACKNOWLEDGED as one of Britain's most accomplished all-round horsewomen, Princess Anne won the ultimate accolade of hardened journalists today when she was named as Sportswoman of the Year by the British Sportswriters Association. She easily headed a poll which included tennis star Virginia Wade and world showjumping champion, Ann Moore.

The 21 year old Princess confirmed her pedigree and class in September, when she won the European Three-Day Event championship at Burghley, on her horse *Doublet*.

Selected as a member of Britain's three-day event team in the 1972 Munich Olympics, Princess Anne would justify her suitability by helping them win gold. For now, she just confessed herself 'stunned, but delighted' with her new title.

NOVEMBER 16

Mao's Heir Dies As China Joins UN

Only hours after mainland Chinese delegates fulfilled their country's long-held ambition to be accepted as an acknowledged member of the international community and took their seats in the United Nations, a power struggle inside China claimed its most notable victim when it was confirmed that Lin Pao - widely believed to be Mao Tse-tung's nominated heir - had been killed in an air crash.

Since Mao stepped back from outright power, apparently content to let his former deputy, Chou En-lai, administer the state as Prime Minister while he remained Chairman of the Communist Party, various factions had reportedly been jostling for future control of the world's most populous nation. Accused of veering away from the party line and a too-close association with the Soviet regime, Lin Pao was actually en route for Russia when his plane blew up in mid-air.

NOVEMBER 18

Queen Meets Rehabilitated Profumo

Seven and a half years after he was forced to quit his British government post when he admitted he'd lied to the House of Commons by saying he had not had an affair with call-girl Christine Keeler, a reformed and rehabilitated John Profumo was accepted back into society today when he greeted the Queen at the official opening of a London docklands residential home.

Secretary of State for War when the Keeler scandal broke, Profumo vanished from the high society circles he and his actress wife Valerie Hobson had once graced and began working full-time for a housing charity in some of London's most deprived areas. It was as a senior figure in that charity that Profumo stepped forward to welcome a smiling Queen Elizabeth and invite her to unveil a commemorative plaque.

NOVEMBER 16

Report Confirms Internee 'Mistreatment'

Accusations that Ulster police and security forces had been mistreating IRA suspects held under internment laws appeared to be confirmed today with the publication of an official government committee report, though it refuted charges of outright brutality.

The committee, headed by Nothern Ireland's ombudsman, Sir Edmund Compton, found that some prisoners were forced to stand for hours at a time while being questioned, while others were subjected to continuous noise and deprived of sleep. They also confirmed that some had been kept in black hoods to complete their disorientation.

Although the committee said it had investigated complaints from 40 internees, only one man actually gave evidence.

ARRIVALS
Born this month:
16: Waqar Younis,
Pakistani Test cricketer

DEPARTURES
Died this month:
16: Junior Parker
(Herman Parker), US blues
singer, writer (*Mystery
Train, Next Time You See
Me*, etc), harmonica player

'Superstar' Takes Sgt Pepper's Crown

An ironic milestone was reached this month when MCA Records announced that the British record for album sales held by The Beatles' *Sgt Pepper's Lonely Hearts Club Band* had finally been beaten, by Jesus Christ Superstar, the controversial musical written by Tim Rice and Andrew Lloyd-Webber. Ironic? It's just that John Lennon once got his old group into very hot water in parts of the US when he was quoted as saying that The Beatles were 'bigger than Jesus' to a lot of people. If MCA are correct, then Jesus has been proved to be bigger than The Beatles at last!

For the record, *Sgt Pepper* had racked up seven million worldwide sales by this time in 1971. *Superstar* had passed the three and a half million figure and, as it was a double album, MCA reckoned that meant it had equalled The Beatles' achievement.

And it was still selling.

Douglas-Home And Smith Sign Rhodesian Peace Deal

SIX YEARS and 13 days after Rhodesia's unilateral declaration of independence (UDI) severed the colony's official links with Britain and led to his country's isolation from normal dealings with the outside world, rebel Rhodesian Prime Minister Ian Smith shook hands with Sir Alec Douglas-Home, the British Foreign Secretary, and signed a deal designed to bring the whole sorry saga to an end.

The agreement aimed to restore Rhodesia's constitutional links with Britain and set a course for legal independence. The European establishment in Rhodesia first declared UDI when the then British government of Harold Wilson made it clear that independence would only be granted if the country's black majority had a voice. Britain's last surviving African colony, Rhodesia was officially ostracized by the world community, though many sanctions imposed on its supply of vital raw materials were beaten with help from the white regime in neighbouring South Africa, and the inventiveness of major international companies who used subsidiaries to continue trading with the rebels.

British opposition leaders pushed Sir Alec to say if the deal resolved the question of the black majority's rights. He confirmed that the settlement would have to be approved 'by the Rhodesian people as a whole' before it was finally ratified.

Jenkins Makes Foot Down In Mouth

A Labour Party election today, to select a new deputy leader for former Prime Minister Harold Wilson, confounded pundits who said that veteran left-winger Michael Foot would win the votes of Parliamentary Labour Party members. His chances were predicted as far better than those of his only opponent, the right-wing Roy Jenkins. He was believed to have destroyed his chances by defying the Party Conference decision to oppose Britain's application for EEC membership and voting with the government last month.

In the event, it was Roy Jenkins who was appointed Wilson's number two.

Fresh Clashes On Indo-Pakistan Border

Full scale war between India and Pakistan became an increased possibility today when a Pakistani military spokesman reported that Indian artillery had begun bombarding the airfield at Jessore, almost 30 miles inside the former East Pakistan, during a second day of heavy fighting.

Meanwhile, the Indian government met in emergency session in New Delhi, to review the situation in the light of an aerial battle in Indian air space when three Pakistani Sabre jets had been shot down.

Pakistan Radio broadcast a statement, saying: 'We have been attacked by India. We are fighting back. We do not know if a state of war exists.'

India Defeats Pakistan In Two-Week War

ONLY HOURS AFTER PROMISING his countrymen that Pakistan's two-week war with India would continue, despite the defeat of its forces in East Pakistan, President Yahya Khan faced reality and announced that he would accept the cease-fire ultimatum he'd been given by Indian Prime Minister, Mrs Indira Gandhi.

As protests at the surrender began spreading through West Pakistan, it became clear that they were aimed as much against him and his military regime as they were mourning the loss of East Pakistan and humiliation by the hated Indians. President Khan would resign three days later, to be succeeded by Prime Minister Ali Bhutto.

In the new Bangladesh, Pakistan's military commander, General 'Tiger' Niazi, tore off his badge of rank and handed his service revolver to Lt General Aurora, the Indian commander. Aurora had allowed Pakistani troops to keep their weapons as defence against packs of resentful locals seeking bloody revenge.

The most violent of these were led by Mukti Fouj guerrillas who had fought alongside the Indian army. Their principal targets were the so-called razakars, who had collaborated with Pakistan, and there were gruesome reports of razakars committing suicide rather than face being torn apart by mobs, as happened to three men caught and killed at the gates of the British High Commission.

The human cost of the war, which would enable the new state of Bangladesh to come into being unhindered, was said to be - for India - a total of 10,633, including 2,307 dead. Pakistani figures were not released, but were believed to be much heavier.

US Distributors Ban 'Obscene' Faces Poster

With 400,000 copies of their new album *A Nod's As Good As A Wink To A Blind Horse*, pressed and ready to hit American recordstores in time for the Christmas rush, British rock star Rod Stewart and his band, The Faces, learned that US distributors were refusing to handle it - a poster included in the sleeve was adjudged obscene!

In Britain, where a different poster had been printed, the album was released - without a hitch - to rave reviews and huge sales. The furore in America meant an inevitable delay, and unexpected holiday jobs for unshockable poster unpackers. Rod and Co would have to wait until 1972 to see the album do just as well in the States. Not that he was over-concerned - with his solo single *Maggie May* and the album on which it featured *(Every Picture Tells A Story)* both riding high in Britain, he was going to have the merriest of Christmases!

DECEMBER 2

Queen 'Surprised' By Pay Rise

The Queen's portion of the Civil List - the money awarded to members of the British Royal Family to pay the salaries and expenses of household staff - was almost doubled today when a study by an all-party Commons select committee recommended that her £475,000 stipend should be increased to a hefty £980,000 ($2,450,000) a year.

Said to have been pleased - and a little surprised - when told of the increase by Prime Minister Edward Heath, the Queen suggested in May that the rising costs of 375 full-time and 100 part-time staff in royal households indicated some investigation. Critics of the system - and the monarchy itself - were quick to condemn what Labour MP Richard Crossman described as 'right regal cheek' when the select committee was first appointed.

UK TOP 10 SINGLES

1: Ernie (The Fastest Milkman In The West)
- Benny Hill

2: Jeepster
- T Rex

3: Coz I Luv You
- Slade

4: Tokoloshe Man
- John Kongos

5: Gypsys Tramps & Thieves
- Cher

6: Theme From 'Shaft'
- Isaac Hayes

7: Something Tells Me (Something Is Gonna Happen Tonight)
- Cilla Black

8: Banks Of The Ohio
- Olivia Newton-John

9: No Matter How I Try
- Gilbert O'Sullivan

10: Till
- Tom Jones

57

DECEMBER 10

Peace Prize For Willi Brandt

A special moment in the long, illustrious and brave career of Willi Brandt (pictured receiving his award from Aase Lionaes), the 58 year old West German Chancellor, today when he was awarded the 1971 Nobel Peace Prize in Oslo. The award was recognition for a lifetime of work dedicated to equality and harmony, both of which had been in short supply during his adulthood. Now 58, Brandt was forced to flee Germany in 1933 as the Nazis targeted him for his stance against their rise. Exiled in Norway and Sweden during WWII, he served as a link with German resistance groups before returning to Germany in 1945. A confirmed socialist, he became a member of the West German parliament, the *Bundestag*, in 1949, and - as mayor of West Berlin from 1957 to 1966 - gained international prominence as a staunch enemy of the Soviet and East German regimes. Elected Chancellor in 1969, he had continued to work tirelessly for reconciliation with the Eastern bloc nations.

DEPARTURES

Died this month:
9: Ralph Johnson Bunche, US diplomat, 1950 Nobel Peace Prize winner
18: Bobby Jones (Robert Tyre Jones), US golf legend

DECEMBER 7

Libya's Gaddafi Siezes BP Holdings

The government of Libya struck at British interests today when it nationalized the £80 million ($200m) local assets of oil giant British Petroleum and withdrew all Libyan deposits from British-owned banks around the world.

Colonel Muammar Gaddafi, Libya's new 29 year old strong-man, said the move was retaliation for Britain's failure to prevent the seizure of three Persian Gulf islands by Iran a few days earlier. Commentators suggested Gaddafi had intended the move all along and the Iranian expedition was only a handy excuse.

World Airlines Threaten Korea Boycott After Fire

ALL MAJOR INTERNATIONAL airlines joined in a threat to ban tourist flights into South Korea today following the deaths of 156 people in a Christmas Day hotel fire in the capital, Seoul. They have demanded that the government ensure that safety measures and rescue equipment regulations are enforced.

Seventy other guests were also injured, some seriously, when fire ripped through the 22-storey Taeyunyak Hotel after a gas cylinder exploded in a second-floor coffee shop and flames cut off guests in higher floors, giving them little chance of escaping the fire and smoke which spread through the two year old hotel.

At least 38 of the dead were killed jumping from upper floors.

Despite its recent construction, the Taeyunyak was not built with exterior fire escapes and contained little in the way of modern fire-fighting appliances. In that respect, it was typical of most Seoul centre hotels. While the threat of an airline ban was revealed, South Korean police said they would issue warrants against the hotel's owners and general manager, charging them with severe negligence.

Grim Christmas As Bombers Hit Ulster

There was little Christmas cheer for the people of Belfast and Londonderry as they tried to do holiday shopping this week. IRA bombers made sure that they, and the security forces, dare not relax as they continued their campaign of intimidation and destruction.

The whole country was outraged when 15 people were killed, and another 13 injured, in a bomb blast which wrecked a Belfast pub, McGurk's Bar. Confusion grew when the British army was forced to deny a Republican MP's allegation that British intelligence agents had carried out the attack.

Others believed that a militant Protestant loyalist group were responsible for the explosion which left 10 men, three women, a girl and a 13 year old boy dead. In a separate outrage, terrorists shot and killed Jack Bernhill, a Stormont senator.

More Mixed Signals From Nixon

The American political scene was in confusion today when President Nixon confirmed that he had ordered the resumption of US bombing raids on targets in North Vietnam. Last month he had pledged to withdraw a further 45,000 US troops from South Vietnam.

Critics of the President's strategy, or apparent lack of strategy, were quick to point out that the North Vietnamese were unlikely to take renewed bombing lying down. The most likely response would be increased attacks from their forces deep in South Vietnam - hardly the ideal time, or situation, for the US to pull more troops out.

YOUR 1971 HOROSCOPE

Unlike most Western horoscope systems which group astrological signs into month-long periods based on the influence of 12 constellations, the Chinese believe that those born in the same year of their calendar share common qualities, traits and weaknesses with one of 12 animals - Rat, Ox, Tiger, Rabbit, Dragon, Snake, Horse, Sheep, Monkey, Rooster, Dog or Pig.

They also allocate the general attributes of five natural elements - Earth, Fire, Metal, Water, Wood - and an overall positive or negative aspect to each sign to summarize its qualities.

If you were born between February 6, 1970 and January 26, 1971, you are a Dog. As this book is devoted to the events of 1971, let's take a look at the sign which governs those born between January 27 that year and January 15, 1972 - The Year of The Pig

THE PIG
JANUARY 27, 1971 - JANUARY 15, 1972
ELEMENT: EARTH   ASPECT: (-)

Pigs, you won't be surprised to learn, have a taste for the good life. They possess a strong sense of luxury, can be extravagant and take great pleasure in pampering themselves and their loved ones. Pigs delight in the stimulation of the senses and enjoying *la joie de vivre*.

Despite this carefree and sensual attitude, Pigs can - when they need to - get stuck into work. Where they're concerned, it's all or nothing. But to compensate for their efforts, they reward themselves with little luxuries, holidays, trips or simply indulging in their favourite leisure pursuits.

This doesn't mean Pigs are frivolous and impractical. On the contrary, they are the most logical and down-to-earth people who may, at times, be considered cool and reserved. Blessed as they are with a paradoxical abundance of composure and self-control, Pigs simply don't allow emotions to cloud the issue.

Pigs love company and social life, adore having fun and - with their light-hearted and sometimes sarcastic attitude

- make amusing company. They find it easy to make friends as people are attracted to their vivacity. They are unpretentious and down-to-earth, and while they can be tactless, this comes from Pigs' essentially honest approach to life. Which means that Pigs are invaluable to have around in peace-making situations.

Some Pigs lack self-reflection and insight, but make up for that with big-hearted generosity which others take advantage of all too often. Though generally tolerant, Pigs can turn vicious when trapped or angered. If they feel their friendship and good nature have been abused, Pigs will dismiss any excuse and simply cut that friendship short.

Pigs put a lot of time and effort into their home life and excel in the culinary arts. When it comes to entertaining, Pigs can be excessive, extravagant and indulgent because they love parties, food, friends and having a good time. They also adore dressing up, and can be accused of showing off. Pigs are basically honest, decent, generous, supportive and trustworthy people who are great to have on your side.

FAMOUS PIGS

Woody Allen
director, writer, actor
HRH The Duchess of York
Julie Andrews
actress, singer
Henry Kissinger
diplomat, Nobel Peace Prize winner
Elton John
singer, songwriter, flamboyant entertainer

John McEnroe
temperamental tennis genius
Ronald Reagan
actor-turned-US President
Tracey Ullman
comic actress, singer
HRH The Duke of Kent
Ben Elton
comedian, scriptwriter, novelist